Summary

Battling Fear with Faith is about the fears which hold us back and prevent us from living the life which could be ours. We all have things we are afraid of, and these fears can be many different things. Fear can create many reactions within us, and we can get stuck in a life of fear living in its shadow. We can get stuck in a rut which is what we except for our lives, but God has an abundant life planned for us. When we build a relationship with God, we can start to see the plans God has in store. In this connection we learn to trust the amount of love God has for us. When we live within this relationship, we can step out of the fear we have been living in. We are able to live in the abundance and love which God has for us.

Battling Fear with Faith

Stepping out in Faith through God's love without Fear

Amber McGlynn

Copyright © 2020 Amber McGlynn

All rights reserved

Publisher: Author Academy Elite

ISBN:
Paperback: 978-1-64746-237-6
Hardback: 978-1-64746-238-3
Ebook: 978-1-64746-239-0

Library of Congress
US Programs, Law, and Literature Division
Cataloging in Publication Program
101 Independence Avenue, S.E.
Washington, DC 20540-4283

Library of Congress Control Number: 2020906970

TABLE OF CONTENTS

Chapter 1: Who We Are in God 1
  Understanding how God sees us

Chapter 2: What Separates us from God? 7
  How not only sin but disobedience can separate us

Chapter 3: Fear 15
  What is fear? Why are we stuck?

Chapter 4: Understanding God's Love 23
  Finding out what God's love means for you

Chapter 5: What is Faith? 28
  Learning what faith is and means

Chapter 6: Trust vs. Faith 35
  How trust plays a role in faith

Chapter 7: Faith vs Fear 41
  How faith can conquer fear

Chapter 8: Stepping Out in Faith 48
  Steps to take to live in faith

Chapter 9: Faith in the Daily 55
  How to live faith in the day to day

PREFACE

Not one person in the world is completely fearless. Small or large, we all have fears of some kind. Each fear can stop us from doing something paralyzing us in a way which nothing else can. It stops us in our tracks, prevents us from moving forward, and causes us to stay where we are.

With all of this standing still and the inability to move forward, we prevent ourselves from experiencing the abundant life which is waiting for us. What is it about fear which puts us in this place where we cannot move? How do we move past this fear, and what is on the other side of fear?

Fear is not of God or how God wants us to live. So, why do we not rely on Him and believe in Him to bring us past our fear into the life He has for us?

In this book, we are going to look at His promises for us, what fear is holding us back from, and how to move forward to live the best life God has for us.

Chapter 1
Who We Are in God

Before we start to understand what separates us from God, when we start to let fear into our lives, we need to understand first who we are in God. We are a unique creation when we are in Him. As a child of God, we have chosen to listen and obey what He has requested of us. Along with this, we have accepted His son, and this alone makes us different in God's eyes. As his children, we are to hold ourselves to a higher standard, as He does. We are set above many others and yet are expected to be with others and to accept others. We are not to see ourselves as better, however, we are to be within the world but out of the world (John 17:16 NKJV). We are made new in God, and we have become his bride, his child and his temple. This combination of things all in one makes us seem complicated (because we are).

One main idea each of these has in common is how each of us is not only loved, preserved, and sacred, we are treasured as well. Now, what I mean by this is we are a treasure to God. He is not only in love with us but will protect us, pursue us, yet still let us be who we are. God will not force his way, but he will still do all of this for us. He lets us decide if we want this type of relationship with Him. It is our choice if we want to seek it. He allows us to be ourselves and is fully satisfied in who we are but wants us to be more. He is ultimately, and wholly in love with us. He desires to be perfectly intertwined with us, so we may fully depend on Him, lean on Him and learn from Him.

So yes, you can say being in a relationship with God is complicated. He made us and then recreated us when we became His child. He wants us to be who we are because He loves us unconditionally, but He also has many desires for our lives as individuals. God wants a strong bond with us and understands it will be unique with each of us. He knows us each distinctively, and speaks to us in our own language, in our distinctive way. Not only is it what He desires for us, but it is what makes God happy. This is why he made us each with our own qualities and the different ways in which we see things and create relationships. If he did not like variety and did not have these qualities himself, then we would not be made in His image as we are.

> GOD DELIGHTS IN US AND OUR UNIQUENESS.

His image means more than merely the physical aspects of what makes us, but everything which constitutes who we are. His image is in our emotions, our mind, our spirit and our soul. We are made as complex people because God is complex. He wants an interconnection with those whom He loves, though none of it is simple. God wants us to learn and grow with Him the way we would in any other relationship. But as with any connection in our lives many things can and do get in the way.

* * *

Each of these descriptions of who we are, are things which are to be loved and respected. For example, His temple is how He describes our bodies once we have accepted Him in our lives.

In 1 Corinthians 6:19-20 (NIV) It says, "Do you not know that your bodies are temples of the Holy Spirit, who is in you, whom you received from God? You were bought with a price, therefore honor God with your bodies."

It is our body as it is, not as we want it to be, for God loves us as we are. He does not want us to all look or to be the same. We are all different for a reason. But our bodies are to be treated with respect and cared for, so we do not break them down. It is important to make sure we understand this. When looking at temples, they are sacred, and well cared for, not simply maintained. They are cared for and preserved with the utmost respect. Each detail is looked at with such care, as an archaeologist when searching for bones tends to them in the gentlest way.

A temple was thought to be the place where God would reside; therefore, this shows our bodies are where the Holy Spirit dwells, and this is where God lives. Not only with us, to speak with us, but in us. When we believe, and voice our belief in God, then the Holy Spirit comes and not only loves us but helps us to live for God and to love God. It takes us as we are. We are to help keep our bodies worthy in many ways. One of these would simply be to take care of ourselves. This can be through our personal health: mental, emotional, physical, and spiritual. If any of these are faulty then our connection to God could be broken. We can have a more difficult time connecting with God not because He chooses to be away or distanced from us, but because when we are not focused on what is healthy, we are focused on what is unhealthy. When we are not aligned and together, we cannot be in line with God.

* * *

We are described many times as the children of God. The sons and daughters of God through our faith in Him and in His son (2 Corinthians 6:18, Romans 8:16, Galatians 4:6 and Galatians 3:26) NIV. These verses confirm we are children of God. Parents are often proud of and love their child. This love is all consuming, and the parent will do anything for their child whom they love. A parent cherishes and adores their child. This is how God sees us. We are His children, and he adores everything about us. He loves our uniqueness; why wouldn't He? He made us. He made us in His image— with emotions, and the ability to love, and choose for ourselves. He created us to love, to have connections, to not be alone, and to enjoy life with others.

* * *

With each of these, there are many ways we are cherished by God. Not only are we cherished and loved, but according to Galatians 4:7 (NLT) where it says, "Now you are no longer a slave but God's own child. And since you are his child, God has made you his heir." We are His heirs and may inherit everything which is of God. As His children, we already have the earth which He made for us and many blessings which he has already given us. As many of us have a child, or know of someone with a child, we can see the love of a good parent. They (the parents) are usually beaming with love and pride in their child and give them many good things. This is how God feels about us, beaming with pride, love, and all good things. He wants to shower us with all of His love as any proud parent would. To some, He may be like a loving father, and others may see Him as a friendly caring mother. However, we view Him He is loving, caring, and patient, wanting nothing but joy and love for our lives.

* * *

This not only shows how we are loved by God, but where he sees us and places us among others. He loves us so much and has placed us above so many things. In Matthew 6:30 it talks about how God has clothed the field, and how much more than this he takes care of you and loves you. When thinking of the amount of love God has for us it reminds me of a child spreading their arms out and saying I love you this much.

WHO WE ARE IN GOD

This was done when Jesus died, his arms were spread apart saying I love you this much. His arms were not only spread and nailed but he never failed us, even when he felt rejected by his own Father, because that is how great His love is. He was able to be separated from His Father to prove His love and to prove we are worth it.

* * *

One of my newest favorite verses is John 10:10 (NKJ) which reads, "The thief does not come except to steal and to kill and to destroy. I have come that they may have life, and that they may have it more abundantly." This verse touches on many different characteristics of both God and Satan. But it also shows we are abundantly loved, and that God has many great things for us. When bad things happen, we often blame God, though the bad things are not of Him as He has many great things for us. When we get stuck on something, or in someplace, we often turn to God and ask why. Often it is not God, it is us, or as in this verse it may be Satan who causes the bad things to happen. He comes to steal, kill, and destroy, where God wants good. We are attracted to the good in God, but we are also tempted by the very nature of Satan.

This verse describes God as a person who wants us to have everything good. He desires us to have not only life but to have it to the fullest, or abundantly. God wants us to be abundant in everything, to have plenty of happiness or joy, to be successful, and so on. There are many blessings and things which God wants us to have. He wants us to reach all of our dreams and to have it all overflowing. God is a gracious and giving God, though there is another part to this verse explaining why we may not reach this bountiful life.

First and foremost, Satan is called a thief, indicating how with Satan everything is stolen or at least not as it may seem. A thief is by nature someone who is in many ways dishonest. They take things which are not theirs by any means necessary, with stealth or with force. Satan takes our hope, dreams, and our resilience to find and achieve the splendid life God has prepared for us. Satan comes in many ways, sneaky ways, to steal this from us. One of Satan's methods which I have experienced, and often seen in others, is this. It takes everything God has for us and tells us it is not reachable or is a lie. This one thing is Fear.

What keeps us from love, or the joy of life? Fear is one of the main reasons we do not live the life and experience the love God has for us. Fear can take on many different forms, and it is what keeps us from moving forward in our lives. We need to work hard to move past fear, because beyond fear, you can find the life which was meant for you. The phrase *fear not,* is mentioned 365 times in the scriptures to remind us to not live in fear. So, we can move past our fears and into the life we are meant to have. Let us break this down and move through how to bring ourselves from fear to our best life.

Chapter 2
WHAT SEPARATES US FROM GOD?

There are a few things which can separate us from God, and from being who we have discovered we are in God. First is sin, another is not becoming a Christian. With this being the most common way in which we are separated from God, it is one of the easier things to move past. Please do not misunderstand me, I'm not saying you will be free of sin and temptation if you believe in God, but you will be fully forgiven for your mistakes.

According to Romans 10:9-10 (AMP):

Because if you acknowledge and confess with your mouth that Jesus is Lord recognizing His power, authority, and majesty as God, and believe in your heart that God raised him from the dead, you will be saved. For with the heart a person believes in Christ as Savior resulting in his justification that is being made righteous- being freed of the guilt of sin and made acceptable to God and with the mouth he acknowledges and confess his faith openly resulting in confirming his salvation.

Therefore, as you can see, it is about changing the heart and letting others know where you now stand. These are the first steps to making us who we are in God so we may enjoy everything God has for us. After taking this step we can begin learning and becoming who we are, entering into a whole new realm. As I said, it does not free us from having committed sin, though it does cover it for us with God because we are covered by Jesus.

* * *

Another way we sin, and distance ourselves, is by disobeying God. This can be in the form of failing to do things which He has asked us to do.

In Ephesians 5:8-10 (AMP):

> *For once you were in darkness, but now you are light in the Lord; walk as children of Light, live as those who are native born to the light, for the fruit the effect, the result of the Light consists in all goodness and righteousness and truth, trying to learn by experience what is pleasing to the Lord and letting your lifestyle be examples of what is most acceptable to Him- your behavior expressing gratitude to God your salvation.*

What this appears to be saying is that we know what God wants and how to behave. We need to behave appropriately in light, or good things, not in dark, or bad things. We are to be an example of God to others, radiating the light of His goodness, and the love which God has for all of his people. We are to be examples, but we cannot do this by holding things against people. By demonstrating love towards everyone, no matter who they are or what they believe, we are able to love others as God loves us. This love of all is possible because He first loved us.

However, this does not mean we have ceased to learn and grow. We are not always going to know right away what it is God wants. If we hear or feel Him speaking to us, telling us something, we need to listen. Though we may not want to

WHAT SEPARATES US FROM GOD?

because it may not be easy to hear, still we may need to hear it. God may be showing us things we do not want to change, but we need to be obedient. We need to listen to what is being said, because when we purposefully do not listen, this is disobedience. When we were younger, we would disobey our parents because we did not like what they were asking us to do. This is what we are doing to God also. He is trying to direct us in the way which is best for us, and we are refusing to listen. This disobedience can place a barrier between us and God preventing us from having the abundance which He has for us.

In Jeremiah 22:21-22 (AMP):

> *I spoke to you in your [times of] prosperity, But you said, "I will not listen!" This has been your attitude and practice from your youth; You have not obeyed My voice. The wind [of adversity] will carry away all of your shepherds (rulers statesmen,) and your lovers (allies) will go into exile. Surely then you will be ashamed and humiliated and disgraced Because of all your wickedness.*

These verses show God values obedience the same as any parent does. With us being His children, we are to obey God as we would obey and respect the things our parents say to us. And this, because we are his Children, after we have confessed and believed in him in the depths of our Heart.

The way in which we act and say things is an indication of what resides in our hearts. Therefore, if God resides in our heart, we should be doing things which would please him, not things that would purposefully hurt him. Though our disobedience can create barriers and prevent the progress we are trying to make within our relationship with God, it will not

> WE MAY PUT UP WALLS AND TRY NOT TO LISTEN TO WHAT GOD IS TRYING TO TELL US, BUT GOD WILL ALWAYS LOVE US.

stop God from loving us. For God is love and will always love his children.

* * *

In Romans 8:37-39 (AMP):

> *Yet, in all things we are more than conquerors and gain an overwhelming victory through Him who loved us [so much that He died for us]. For I am convinced [and continue to be convinced— beyond any doubt] that neither death, nor life, nor angels, nor principalities, nor things present and threatening, nor things to come, nor powers, nor height, nor depth, nor any other created things will be able to separate us from the [unlimited] love of God, which is in Christ Jesus our Lord.*

These verses cover several different concepts with many important things to look at within each verse.

First is God's unfailing love which nothing we do can take away. This is another example of a characteristic we have inherited from God. It is something we have which is a reflection of His image within us. We are made from love and for love, as with any other close relationship. Something else which is brought to our attention by this set of verses is God's understanding. We will not lose His love once we accept Him and believe in our heart of hearts, He is who He says he is.

This is fundamentally why God created us— to have a relationship, an-ever developing deep bond. This relationship can be seen as we are called to be His children.

In 1 John 3:1 (AMP) it says, "See what an incredible quality of love the Father has shown to us, that we would [be permitted to] be named *and* called *and* counted the children of God! And so, we are! For this reason, the world does not know us, because it did not know Him." Again, we are shown how we are in a parental relationship with God.

WHAT SEPARATES US FROM GOD?

God knows we are growing and learning as any child does, but this takes time. He is forgiving and nothing can completely keep us from Him. God knows we stumble and fall, but if we are able to admit when we are wrong and confess these things which make us stumble as we make progress in defeating our faults, nothing will stop God from loving us. He still wants good for us, and has amazing plans for us, because He knows us and holds us in great regard.

* * *

God came as Jesus to show us love, and to accept us as we are. With this it means to accept our flaws, and our downfalls while continuing to love us. He made the conscious choice to love beyond all as it says in these verses, and in the actions of sending His son. In 1 John 4:7-8 (AMP) it says, "Beloved, Let us [unselfishly] love *and* seek the best for one another, for love is from God; and everyone who loves [others] is born of God and knows God [through personal experience]. The one who does not love has not become acquainted with God [does not and never did know Him] for God is love. [He is the originator of love and it is an enduring attribute of his nature.]" This shows God is the one who has given all love to all. He wants us to love all in the same way in which He has loved us. To know His love also means to share his love with anyone. To love anyone is not to judge them but to accept them.

* * *

Back to Romans 8:37-39 where another thing these verses bring to light is the knowledge of when God is on our side we are able to do anything. We are able to conquer anything which is standing in our way whether it be fear, self-doubt, or anything else. With God on our side we are made to gain victory for God will direct us in the way in which we are to do this. God has great plans for those who Love him as He loves them. These verses go through a list of many things which people think can keep us from God and experiencing His love. These are things which can keep us from having a fulfilled life and living our dreams. But one thing to consider is God's love is given freely to us; all we have to do is acknowledge him and accept it. We have to confess our God as who He is, but really that is all which is keeping His love from us. We stand in our own way because we do not think it is for us, but it is. He wants us as we are, mistakes, future mistakes and all. We are his children, and He wants to cherish us. Though many people read Isaiah 1:14-19 and think God will turn from them forever and even stop loving them, this is not how He operates.

In Isaiah (AMP) it says,

> *I hate [the hypocrisy of] your New Moon festivals and your appointed feasts. They have become a burden to Me; I am weary of bearing them. So when you spread out your hands [in prayer, pleading for My help], I will hide My eyes from you; Yes, even though your offer many prayers. I will not be listening. Your hands are full of blood! Wash yourselves, make yourselves clean; Get your evil deeds out of My sight; Stop doing evil, Learn to do good, Seek justice, Rebuke the ruthless, Defend the fatherless. Plead for the [rights of the] widow [in court]. Come now, and let us reason together, Says the Lord. Though your sins are like scarlet, They shall be white as snow, Though they are red like crimson, They shall be like wool. If you are willing and obedient, You shall eat the best of the land.*

These verses go over many different things. They show how many people have done evil things and yet God is still willing to love them. It says if one is to continue to be in His love after having disobeyed or done evil, one is to confess and be willingly obedient. These verses in Isaiah show how even in the old testament people had chosen to disobey, and God still loved them.

These verses also indicate how when we disobey, or are evil, we are placing a barrier between us and God. He reveals this by refusing to listen to their cries or prayers while they continue in their disobedience. So, yes, we can create barriers between us and God, but He will never stop loving us. We are his children, and love is what God is. We have learned to love because we have experienced love. Love being the main characteristic of God, we have love because of God.

Once we accept and declare God in our lives, we are never alone. We may block Him, but we never lose him. God will not abandon you no matter what you do. He may stop listening and talking, but He is always in reach. It is our job and has always been our choice as to how much of a relationship we want to have with Him. This is another of the beauties of God; He has given us free choice. We choose how close we are to Him. We can decide to tell him little to nothing and allow Him to save us, or we can strive for something deeper— the bond we all crave. The desire to know and be truly known is yet another characteristic of God; it is our desire for connection which makes us like him.

According to James 4:8 (AMP): "Come close to God [with a contrite heart] and He will come close to you. Wash your hands, you sinners; and purify your [unfaithful] hearts, you double-minded [people]." This verse discusses how, when we desire to come close to God with a remorseful heart, He will draw near to us. With this in mind when we come to God, knowing we've done wrong or having disobeyed Him, we know He is still willing to be near us. He is understanding, but we also need to be willing to admit when we are at fault as well. When we open up with God (our parent) and admit our shortcomings then this starts to build a healthy relationship with Him. The more we build a healthy positive relationship with God, the more this will flow into other parts of our lives.

The more we hold up our end the more we will figure out what our abundant and fulfilled life can be like. Though this is not the only thing we have to do to build a close connection, it's a start. As with any relationship there are many factors which come into play. Being willing to be in this relationship and holding up our end is obviously the first and most important step. So, before we continue, is this something you are willing to do? Let's work on us, and take the steps needed to move forward toward the life which is waiting for us, in God's love and His plan for us.

CHAPTER 3
FEAR

Fear, a four-letter word which can do and mean so much. The very word can bring about the thing one is actually afraid of. It invokes images to the forefront of one's mind, such as spiders, snakes, failure, being alone and so on. Fear can have such a strong hold on us and the way we react to things. In fact, fear creates a biological reaction, called the fight or flight instinct.

The fight or flight instinct is a hormonal reaction which has many biological manifestations. This is revealed in the physical expressions of a racing heart, widened visual perception, and increased respiratory rate (breathing). Fear can also create other complications throughout your body. Problems such as digestive difficulties, increased heartbeat, and feelings of weakness, in addition to the physical, mental, and emotional strain, even leading up to depression. These feelings can block us from proceeding in life and can get us stuck in a cycle of negativity.

The stress of being afraid, or anxious all the time, will take a toll on a person in every aspect. It can drain you physically, emotionally, or psychologically which can make it difficult to function normally. Then because you are so fatigued you dwell on this fear even more and all you can do is sit there having been drained of your energy. When this is all you dwell on it becomes the new normal of your life. I know this may seem ordinary to you if it is what you are going through, but this should not be your normal. This is why many people live in a stress bubble; however, you do not need to. You are meant for more.

Sometimes the fear which consumes your life becomes who you are. The thing you are afraid may happen actually does because, for lack of better words, you willed it to happen. You became so consumed in the what if's and the how's of your fear it all came to pass. I know, because it happened to me.

Literally, I was lying in bed one morning snuggling my kids and praying when the words *Battling Fear with Faith* came to my mind. I was like um ok, pushed it aside, and went about my day. Those words continued to pop into my head all day, so finally I gave in. I prayed, "God what do you want me to do?" With those words, I gave in to Him and it was like, what do you want from me. The next word that came to mind, or rather more of flashed across my mind was *write*. I was all dumbfounded, I have not written anything remotely like that before. I have no idea what I am doing, I am not trained, I am a nurse. I write for me and my own pleasure. Plus, I have not written anything in years. All those thoughts went through my mind as I envisioned the word *write*. I started to feel my heart race, and I said to myself, "*No* I can't do this." This is not for me. I started to argue with myself and with my fear of doing something *big* for God. I don't do this kind of thing. I started to let the fear of stepping out and doing a *big* thing for God take over. Then I told myself, "Nope, I am imagining this." I cleared my head and gave myself over to God again (because I was trying to tell myself He doesn't really want *me* to do that), but again, the word *write* came across my mind. So, I told God, "Ok, but I have no idea what I am doing." Each time I have sat down to write, God has shown me more. It was more about myself, my personal fears, and how to let them go, as well as how to break through the cages I have put on myself.

FEAR

God has shown me what He wants in this book and what He wants me to share with you. The more I write for Him, the more I am able to step out of my fears and back into faith.

Throughout the process, I've had many different reasons to hesitate. I even stopped writing for fear of not knowing what I was to write, of messing it up, of it not being what God wanted. All of these concerns caused me to stop, ceasing the progress which He wanted me to make, but over the many years which it has taken me to write this book, God has shown me the way. I have learned about myself in more depth and about the power fear has which can take hold of a person. It can interfere in your life, even when you are doing your best to live a life for God. Living and working with God does not make you immune to what Satan may be doing to stop you from succeeding. Satan will do whatever he can to block you from completing the path to your abundant life.

* * *

So, let me tell you first off, you are not alone when experiencing fear. Everyone is afraid of something. I am personally afraid of failing. This is not something which shows up on the outside, but it is very real and sometimes paralyzing when it comes to my ability to change. Hopefully you can imagine the level of fear I faced when it finally hit me, not only was I unhappy as a nurse but I was about to change careers and go back to school again in the totally different field of Psychology. I was facing a new challenge in which I truly could fail. Not to mention, on top of going to school, I was writing this book which in itself brought on even more anxiety. The thoughts which ran through my head most of the time when I thought of writing were, I have no idea what I am doing, I am not qualified, and what am I trying to do here.

Some of those questions were answered right away by the Holy Spirit, others God merely showed me as the writing began to flow. God made it His own work with His words flowing from me onto the pages. I look back at times and am like *Wow* where did that come from. At times I'd think was I really supposed to write that? Most of the time I leave it alone because I can see as I read it God makes it all work together. When He wants something done, He makes it happen. The Holy Spirit reminds me too, I am here to help, I am a voice to show people God's love. That in itself helps keep me motivated to write.

With going back to school, I am reminded daily of my desire to help, and how God has his hand on everything and is guiding me. Though I may not see it right away He is always there and shows up in little ways. Though it may be subtle I watch for these reminders of Him. It may be little reminders of why I am done with Nursing, or an affirmation in my heart while I explain to someone why it is, I am getting out of nursing. God is always found in the still small whisper of our hearts. Take time to ponder and talk with Him today, but don't do all the talking, take some time to be quiet and listen. It may be on the drive to work, before everyone gets up, or even in the shower. Talk, but then stop and wait for His voice in your heart and mind to guide you. He waits for us to be still, to stop talking.

When we do not take the time to commune with God it can become a vicious cycle, until we realize we need to do something positive to get out of the negative rut we have gotten ourselves into. How do we do this? First, we need to move past the self-doubt, and realize there is something better for us. If you can acknowledge this for a few seconds then you can remind yourself daily of the verse in Jeremiah 32:27 (NIV) where it says, "I am the Lord, the God of all mankind. Is anything too hard for me?" With this not only is God reminding us of who He is, He is also pointing out how he has everything in His hands. He has amazing power. He holds us in his arms and protects us from everything we fear. We only need to look to Him. Though it may be a fear of letting God or family down, He knows this and chooses to love you through it. God is bigger than any fear; you simply have to lean on Him. It may not feel like it, but His shoulders are big enough to handle it.

The more I write this book for Him, the more I am able to see this is bigger than me or my fear. In fact, this is not even about me or us as individuals, but rather what God has for us all.

God may not ask something of you of this magnitude, but whatever you feel He is saying to you I encourage you to step back and take time for Him. Confirm what he wants and do it for Him. God will reward you each and every time. With me the reward is the words flowing out of me allowing me to conquer my fears of judgement and failure as I go. He may be asking you something simple.

> GIVE GOD WHAT HE ASKS EVEN IF IT IS LITTLE, AND HE WILL REWARD YOU WITH MUCH.

For example, look at the parable of the talents in Matthew 24:21,23. In the parable, the master had entrusted the servants with different amounts of talents (a large amount of silver or gold, worth a large amount of money). Both the servants who had multiplied the talents were praised, celebrated, and entrusted with more. However, the servant who had received only one talent and did nothing with it was thrown out and not allowed to celebrate. Now think of this with how God responds to you. Do you want to be trusted to help grow God's kingdom? Do you want to do more for God? Are you hungry to help? If so, show God you can be trusted with a little, and He will give you much.

This is another verse to meditate on once you get some down time. I want you to use it to remind yourself of who you are in God. 1John 4:18 (NLT) says, "Such love has no fear, because perfect love expels all fear. If we are afraid it is for fear of punishment, and this shows that we have not fully experienced his perfect love." He made us as we are. We are perfect images of what He wants us to be. It is not our love which should drive out fear or the love of others accepting us as we are, but it is God's love which should drive out our fear. It should drive out our fear of failure, and fear of unworthiness.

In Isaiah 43:1-2 (NLT), it says

> *But now, O Jacob, listen to the Lord who created you. O Israel, the one who formed you says, Do not be afraid, for I have ransomed you. I have called you by name; you are mine. When you go through deep waters, I will be with you. When you go through rivers of difficulty, you will not drown. When you walk through the fire of oppression, you will not be burned up; the flames will not consume you.*

These verses use many different analogies in which fear or other things may overwhelm you. It talks about many different ways in which God will protect you, as you are His child. He cares about you and wants nothing but the best for you. As God calls Jacob by his new name, the personal name Israel, God almost seems to use it as a nickname or pet name for Jacob. This shows the personal relationship which they have. This is the type of relationship God has and wants for you too. To help you to have this closeness with God you have to work on the concept of *do not be afraid*. When we are afraid and do not think of or believe in this relationship, we prevent this relationship.

Another verse showing how much God is on our side is Psalms 118: 5-6 where it says, "In my distress I prayed to the Lord, and the Lord answered me and set me free. The Lord is for me, so I will have no fear. What can mere people do to me?" These verses are a few of many verses which show God does not want negative, fearful, distressful, outcomes for us. God wants nothing but good for us. He has great and amazing plans for us.

In John 10:10 (AMP) this is specifically stated, "The thief comes only in order to steal and kill and destroy. I came that they may have and enjoy life, and have it in abundance (to the full, till it overflows)." With these two verses it shows God has great plans for us, beyond what we can imagine. What is preventing these from being fulfilled, is considered the thief, Satan. Satan can stop us dead in our tracks with fear. Satan will do, and does, anything he can think of to stop us from fulfilling God's purpose. Satan would rather us live in fear than in the abundance which God has in store for us. Therefore, he plants seeds of doubt and fear within us to impede our progress.

Through this verse we are shown how if we call to God, if we reach out, He is always there. We just have to be honest about what is holding us back. We have to cry out to God with our whole heart, and He will come and help us.

This is explained perfectly in Jeremiah 29:12&13 (AMP):

Then you will call on Me and you will come and pray to Me, and I will hear [your voice] and I will listen to you. Then [with a deep longing] you will seek Me and require Me [as a vital necessity] and [you will] find Me when you search for Me with all your heart.

This shows God wants us to know deep within how much we need Him. We cannot get to where He wants us without Him. He is the key to truly overcoming the fear which is stopping us.

He wants us to long for his help, and many of us do, but for different reasons we may also be fearful of asking for his help. I know I was less afraid of asking for His help, but more afraid of being let down. This stemmed from being let down in many ways by people. People had shown me over the years how I was not important enough or worthy of their help. I had pushed this belief on to God despite the many times His word had shown how if we seek Him, He is there to be found. So, reach out and listen to your inner self. You need to find your fear and confess it to God. Reach out to God and ask Him how He wants you to conquer your fear. As we listen to what God has planned for us He may show this to us in many different ways, we just need to be open to them. God may speak to us by reminding us of a verse or a quote which can speak to us as individuals. If we do not listen we will live with anxiety, starting a vicious cycle of fear and unhappiness. This is not what God has in store for us.

In Jeremiah 29:11-13 (NKJV):

> *For I know the thoughts that I think toward you, says the Lord, thoughts of peace and not evil, to give you a future and a hope. Then you will call upon Me and go and pray to Me, and I will listen to you. And you will seek Me and find Me, when you search for Me with all of your heart.*

These verses declare not only does God have no desire for you to live in fear, but He also has good plans and thoughts for you, thoughts of peace and hope. Living with fear does not come from Him, it comes from Evil, or Satan, as Satan is the thief who comes to steal and destroy. Fear does not come from anything which God wants for us, but Satan uses fear as a way to prevent us from being exactly who God has planned for us to be.

The more we struggle and live in this fear, the more we put off our purpose and what is planned for us. An amazing idea which speaks to this exact concept is …The more we argue with our fear, the more of that is what we get. (paraphrased from Melissa Gilbert) This saying is referring to our limitations, though it can be related to our fears as well. This idea shows the more we ponder on fear, anxiety, or moving forward, the more reasons for our concern will come to pass. Anxiety and fear create a life unlike the one which God desires for you. He wants you to have a life wherein you can thrive, have hope, and live a life of overflowing abundance.

Chapter 4
Understanding God's Love

Though many things hold us back, God has a thriving and abundant life set aside for us within his love. When we understand and live within the Love of God, we feel His presence more often than before. When we live in God's presence, and love, we know more of what God's plans are for us. He starts to show us the steps we must take to live the life which He has planned for us.

Before we get into the ways God loves us, I want to explain how there are many (eight in fact) different types of love which can be expressed. According to the ancient Greeks, these are Eros, Philia, Storage, Ludus, Mania, Pragma, Agape, and Philautic. Eros is an erotic love, Philia is an affectionate love, Storage is a familiar love, Ludus is playful love, Mania is an obsessive love, Pragma is an enduring love, Agape is a self-less love and Philautic is a selflove. The English language only has one-word *love* to explain all of these forms.

As we have seen God's love, any love really, comes in many different forms and is expressed in different styles. One way we talked about briefly is Mania, Mania is thought to be a crazy, over the top love; a jealous, only mine type of love. Though there is nothing to fully show that God has this type of love for us, I believe He is over the top in love with us, there are a few verses that discuss God as a jealous God.

Nonetheless, without being able to talk to God, or even know the true context of these verses, it is hard to say exactly where this jealousy is coming from. I like to think it comes from His love for us and God wanting to be first in our lives. But again, nothing really says it is from this place. I think this way because I know of God's love and the ways He views us, and how he has said He wants no one before Him in our lives. He wants us to come to Him first, to be the first person we talk to when things are rough, or even to thank Him first when things are good. So, to know if God has the Mania type of love for us, well we will never truly know but we do know of the many other ways He loves us.

Along with the fact that God loves us to the extreme, meaning the love he has for us and things He wants for us is the best of the best for us. God is captivated with us (Agape, Philia, Pragma) and selflessly loves us as we are, wanting only the finest things for us. God knows us as individuals and affectionately works things in our favor to help within our lives.

I know it is hard to believe that God, the one above everything, can be obsessed with us as individuals, but God loves us more than we can imagine. He is enthralled to have a relationship with us (Storage) and He did whatever He could (giving up his son) to ensure *we* could have a thriving connection with Him. By doing this He ensured we could have the familiar love (Storage) with Him, opening up a way to have a familiar and open relationship with Him.

Though stepping out in faith is the goal, it is hard to achieve if you do not understand the Love which God has for you. In 1 John 4:9-10 (NLT) it says, "God showed how much he loved us by sending his one and only Son into the world so that we might have eternal life through him. This is real love—not that we loved God, but that he loved us and sent his Son as a sacrifice to take away our sins." I want you to truly think about the depths of this. I know we have all heard many times how Jesus was sent to die for us. Jesus was God's only son and was sent to die on the cross. This thought process did not truly hit me with its full depth until I became a mother.

One night while reading those words in 1John 4:9-10 (NLT) it truly hit me. God gave up his son. He was separated from him for 30 plus years while Jesus was on earth. I don't know about you but being away from my kids for more than 2 days is hard. Then to know the reason His son was here on earth. To watch His only Son, go through life and then die and surrender Him. I cannot imagine that amount of Pain. All because He loved us. He did all of this so we would know the extent of His love. Not because we would eventually love Him but because He loved us already. He loved us before we were even born. He knew us and loved us.

Let's review a concept which was mentioned in the beginning of this book. To understand the love God has for us we must first understand we were created in the image of God. It tells us this in the First book and first Chapter of the Bible. In Genesis 1:27 (NLT) it says, "So God created human beings in his own image. In the image of God, he created them, male and female He created them."

So, we are of the image of God and we are loved by God just as we are. Fear may take over but for me just knowing God created me as I am helps to relieve some of the rising anxiety. God loves me as I am. I can be who I am, as I am, and He is pleased with me. That in itself is encouraging. Fear is always there. Whether it is a fear of spiders, of failure, or fear of loneliness, it is there. It is a part of our lives. But look for comfort in knowing God, knowing his love, and battling that fear (whatever it may be) in His love while having the knowledge we are made in His image. A reminder that we have God's Love and are made exactly how He wants us to be. Remember, He made us special for whatever purposes He has meant for only us to fulfill. You are designed to be the way you are for a reason. To be this person, we need to move past this fear and grasp what God's love is truly like. It took me some time to fully accept and feel the full extent of God's love.

I will never forget when I first felt the full extent of God's love. The first time was when I became a Christian. I remember so clearly— like it happened yesterday. I was only a teenager and did not fully understand what I was experiencing. I remember praying, feeling like I had failed, like I was nothing to no one. I didn't feel like I could accomplish anything. As I lay on my bed in the fetal position, I felt as though someone (God) had picked me up, placed me in His lap, and told me while stroking my hair, "I love you just as you are. You are my daughter." I opened my eyes. I was crying, overwhelmed, and could not move. No one else was around.

Another time I remember feeling all of this was, again, at a low point of my life quite recently. I was starting to write this book and feeling inadequate. I had bought a ticket to women's conference at my church. I did not want to go due to feeling down and not knowing anyone else who was going, but my loving husband had convinced me to go. The first night I was there (it was a two-night conference), one of the speakers was talking about not feeling loved, or like you deserved to be loved. Specifically, by a father, not knowing what a father's love was truly like. Little backstory on me, I am a child of divorce, my real father saw me out of duty, and my step dad and I did not get along most of my life, though we are starting to get along now since I have become an adult and have a family of my own. Anyways, so I never truly felt the love and protection of a father and had always felt like that was taken from me. As she was talking I felt this burden on my heart to let go of my resentment. I tried to argue, but as you know that is not the easiest thing to do with God. The need to let all of it go, (the pain, resentment, and anger) was overwhelming. The speaker asked the women who had not had that love to stand, then encouraged the woman around the people who had stood, to hug them. As I was being hugged I felt that burden lift and this feeling of acceptance, love, and praise fell over me. I was so taken over by this I was in tears and had almost fallen to my knees.

That is how powerful the love of God can be. Those events truly changed me, and made me look at life and love differently. It helped with my anger because I no longer felt the need to prove something. Don't get me wrong there are still times where God's love feels far away but I know all I have to do is pray and let God know I accept His love and he breaks down the walls again. That is it, all you have to do is to have an open heart and mind and the love comes pouring in. God wants us to want him. In John 11:22 (NLT) it states, *"But even now I know that God will give you whatever you ask."* It is literally that simple, we need to ask and God will shower down His love on us, so much so we cannot keep it to ourselves. Part of what we are called to do is share God's love, because it is so great. As it says in Matthew 22:38-39 (NLT) "This is the first and greatest commandment. And the second is equally important: Love your neighbor as yourself." So we are called to share the Love of God, as it is such a great gift. A gift we can receive by asking with no other strings attached.

Our hearts have to be open. This love God has for us is overwhelmingly pleasant and a wonderful warm place to reside. Have you taken the time to not just invite Him in your life but to be open to His love. You also have to come expecting to be filled. Honestly it is crazy the way His love reaches into the places which you thought you had closed off to others. Personally when God poured out His love on me it was so overwhelming I cried. This may not happen for everyone as everyone experiences emotions and things within their spirit differently. But I encourage you to be open and willing for anything. God's love is an amazing thing, let him share this with you.

> THE GIFT OF THIS LOVE IS SOMETHING WE RECEIVE ONLY WHEN WE ARE READY FOR IT.

Chapter 5
WHAT IS FAITH?

We have defined fear so now let us define faith. Faith is confidence or trust in something or someone, a belief not based on proof. These are a few of the definitions. Belief is often interchanged for faith, though these can be seen differently. Belief is simply accepting something could be real, where Faith is knowing it with your whole being. Faith is knowing, not just simply accepting something as real. Faith is taking the belief a step further than simple acceptance. Faith is a combination of belief, knowledge and confidence in something or someone.

So, it takes belief to have faith. Many times in the Bible we are told to have childlike faith or belief (Matthew 18:2-4). To me when this is talked about I think of having an imaginary friend. I think of this because no one can see them but you. To you, your imaginary friend is real. As a child you tell them everything and they are everywhere with you. It is so real to you that you can tell them everything and know they will share none of it with anyone. You name your imaginary friend, and you share your biggest fears with them. You take them with you everywhere you go. No one else may know they are there, but you do. You see them, you feel them hug you when you are scared. They are treasured by you and you

WHAT IS FAITH?

feel a comfort when they are around you. You know they love you just the way you are.

Now think of that imaginary friend and everything they meant to you. Just as God is omnipresent, your make-believe friend is with you at all times as well. He knows everything and you can tell him everything. We need to have faith or confidence in God that He will be there for us, as a child does with their imaginary friend.

Believing and having faith in God is not always easy. Knowing He loves you makes it easier. As we discussed in the previous chapter, God has an overwhelming love for us. We as individuals are his world. In 1 John 4:19 (NIV) it says, "We love because He first loved us." Without knowing this love, it is hard to get past the fear and move to trusting and having faith as God wants us to. The more we allow ourselves to accept this love, and try to live in this love, the more we will be able to have Faith and confidence God will always be there for us. As we are always there to help those we love, God is always there for us. He is there to pick us up and to shower us with His love.

* * *

Being made in God's image is why we are made for relationships. We are made from love; to be loved and to love others. We are made for this connection, and with any relationship comes a faith and confidence within the other person in the association.

> THE MORE WE GET TO KNOW AND EXPERIENCE GOD THE MORE THE FAITH WILL COME.

Now let us think— how do we get passed this fear? Other than merely living in the overwhelming love given so freely to us, we must gain confidence and faith in God. We need to change something so we are no longer living in fear or it will be our life. Let us look at one thing which may help us move past the fear. It is called faith. The confidence which we have in each other as people shows how easily people can earn our faith. If we can have this level of hope in people, why then is it so hard to have faith in God? If we can have faith, confidence, and belief in people to do the right thing, why do we have so little in God? If we as individuals are made in God's image why is this faith not extended to God also? Many of these questions plague me daily. Conclusions I have come to are simply it is this way because we do not have a real relationship with God. We do not know Him like we know the people who we surround ourselves with daily. Another may be since we cannot physically see God, and how much He cares for us, it makes Him less real for us. So this brings about the questions discussed in Luke 11:13 (AMP) which says, "If you, then, being evil, [that is, sinful by nature,] know how to give good gifts to your children, how much more will your heavenly father give the Holy Spirit to those who *ask* and continue to ask Him!"

In other words, if we know how to have confidence in others to do good things, how come we cannot do the same with God? If we are created in His image, and the image of His character, then we received from God how to give good and positive gifts. If we, with only a fraction of his character have this desire, and can give good things, think of how much more God can and does give to us.

The kicker is we can't merely think on this; we have to believe it. We have to have the confidence and faith that this, too, is what God will do for us. As we would do these things for others, He too will do these things for us. As it says in Luke 11:10 and 1 John 5:14 we have but to ask. Not only must we ask, but we must also ask with faith, confidence, and the expectation that this will come to us, or if it does not, than God has something better for us. We have to have the Faith God will do good for us, even when we may not understand the how or why. To build on this and gain this understanding, all within faith, we need to gain an understanding of who God is.

WHAT IS FAITH?

Faith and belief doesn't require a relationship, however, to have this will help breed faith. Faith can also come from reading and learning about God. Though it does not take much faith to have God show his plan to you, it requires consistent faith to live this daily. To have this faith and to have full confidence in God, is to show yourself fully to him. Such as the verse in Matthew 13:31 (AMP) which says, "He gave them another parable to consider saying, the kingdom of heaven is like a mustard seed, which a man took and sowed in his field."

This uses a mustard seed as an example because the mustard seed is one of the smallest seeds, but it is also one of the fastest growing herbs. So, this is saying that when one has Faith in God, it can grow quickly like the mustard seed. It is not necessarily a degree or amount of faith which can move a mountain it is simply pure faith as it grows.

Another well-known story of the mustard seed which is a parable in Matthew 17:20 (AMP) where it says, "He answered, Because of your little faith, [your lack of trust and confidence in the power of God]; for I assure you *and* most solemnly say to you, if you have [living] faith the size of a mustard seed, you will say to this mountain, 'move from here to there' and [if it is God's will] it will move; and nothing will be impossible for you" Many people look at this verse and think faith comes in all different sizes but I think this verse is used for a few different reasons. First not to show sizes of faith, but what living faith is, to daily trust and have a relationship with God. It is this kind of faith which can move mountains. It also shows God still has a say in our lives as well. It uses the mustard seed, which we have learned is a fast growing potent plant, as an example. With this knowledge true faith is like a mustard seed, fast growing, wanting to grow. This verse also shows it will happen if it is God's will for you, but if it is not we must still have *faith* or *confidence* that God only wants good things for us. With all of this we learn when we have a relationship with God, we know God.

With any level of faith, the seed must be planted, and to be a true faith we must grow, learn, and be planted in God. As any seed has to be planted to grow, so does our faith. It grows and sprouts into the vast plant it can be, gaining the relationship with God, which is building off of everything we have talked about encompassing God's love. Live in God's overwhelming love and experience it. Build a relationship with God and get to know who He is; learn about what He has done.

So, let's get a little personal: what is holding you back? If you are anything like me, I have a problem trusting in general as I have been let down by many people in my life. The concept of having faith without any proof is difficult for me. As I have been writing this book however, God has shown me this about myself. As I have learned more about him and what he has done, I have seen a change in myself. While writing this book, building a relationship, and being open to what He wants to say, I have learned more about God and myself.

Now, I don't want you to think I am saying this is the only way to get to know God. This is what worked for me which is the beauty of being unique and individual. God knows each of us and how to communicate with us. As I continue to do things for Him, He calls me to other things. God may not have something this big in store for you. God knows you, what you are capable of, and what talents you have, but He wants to expand those. To do so, and to live the life he has for us, we have to have confidence and faith in Him. Within this relationship of faith, you will see Him working and exposing things to you. The more you are open with him about everything, like the imaginary friend we talked about, the more He will not only listen but remove the obstacles and place things in your life which can only be from Him.

An example of this would be how I was able to find the time to write this book. I was working full-time as an HR director for a company, had very little down time and was

WHAT IS FAITH?

tired when I got home. I did not have time to write (which I truly enjoy doing). After about a year of this, I was let go from that position. Needless to say I was devastated; I enjoyed my work. Once again found myself in the nursing field, which I was continually trying to get out of. This time felt different though as I started to use my time for what I enjoyed and started writing this book. The more I dedicated my time to the book, the more it came together. Then in January of 2019, I found a Facebook ad for Author Academy Elite. I went through part of their program, and as they learned about me and my book they agreed to have me in their full program. I have been blessed, and looking back I can see it was all in God's plan. I don't want to continue in nursing but it has given me time to do what I enjoy and complete this book.

We have confidence God has a plan for good and hope for us when we cry for Him, from the depths of our heart, believing He will bring it all to fruition. In Jeremiah 29:11-12 (AMP) it says, "For I know the plans and thoughts that I have for you," says the Lord, "plans for peace *and* well-being and not for disaster, to give you a future and a hope. Then you will call on Me and you will come and pray to me, and I will hear [your voice] and I will listen to you." So this verse shows how we can have faith God has good and not bad planned for us. Not only does it speak of this, it also reveals He listens to us and hears our individual voices. He is in such a loving, caring, deep relationship with us He knows our voice.

Think about this— God knows our voice above all others because He knows us intimately— like a spouse, or other family member. With the knowledge of this love, how can you not have faith in His wanting good things for you as any other family member or spouse would. We have confidence in them to bring good, and to help our dreams and plans come to fruition, how can we not have confidence in God? It simply comes down to trust. Trust is different from faith and confidence, and it is the next concept we will dive into.

BATTLING FEAR WITH FAITH

Not an easy subject but a very important one all the same. Without trust we cannot have a successful relationship with anyone, including God.

Chapter 6
Trust vs. Faith

Trust and Faith— they go together. Trust is specifically seen as a belief in the reliability, truth, or even the strength of someone or something. Faith is the act of having confidence and knowledge in something or someone. In the relationship we build with God, faith and trust start to be seen as one. These two things, faith and trust, go hand in hand. As your faith grows and your relationship with God blossoms, your trust in God will grow as well.

Though trust is usually automatically given to a person when you are in a relationship with them, as soon as it is lost or broken it takes a while to rebuild. As we continue to talk about trust and we dive into this, we will be reminded of the difficulty of this subject. Stay with me and we will figure this trust thing out together.

* * *

Trust is not an easy subject, and it is a common struggle among many people including myself. I often have a hard time trusting people I deal with, and at times an even harder time Trusting God. I am not a person who trusts blindly. Most of the time I have to be shown I can trust someone with small things before I can trust them with bigger things. This is because there is a fear which comes with trusting in someone, or perhaps it is more a fear of being let down. If you trust and believe in someone, and things do not go the way you were thinking they would you are naturally let down and disappointed.

* * *

I have heard many people use the example of trusting a chair when you go to sit down, and they try to liken this to the trust we should have in God. To me these are very different for one because I can see the chair and feel the chair. Plus, when I look around I can ensure no one is there to pull it out from underneath me. So, how is this similar to our trust in God? I often think to myself; I do not see God with my physical eyes and can't touch him with my hands. I feel Him with a sense, but not one of the five senses I use to assure myself in the physical world. It is more of an internal sense, almost like a gut instinct that things will be fine, or that He has my back. More times than not, when looking back at difficult times in my life, or even over my life in general, I can see little touches of God in places where I didn't know he was there, but in the moment it was the more difficult part.

* * *

In Psalms 56:11 (AMP) it states, "In God have I put my trust and confident reliance; I will not be afraid. What can man do to me?" When we have absolute trust in someone we may feel as though anyone other than them can hurt us. For me it can be difficult to trust when I cannot and do not see God moving in my life. I completely understand this difficulty which many people face. It is hard to trust when you can't always see the results, though this is another aspect of trusting in God which makes it all the more beautiful.

In Proverbs 3:5 (AMP) it states, "Trust in and rely confidently on the Lord with all your heart and do not rely on your own insight or understanding." We should not rely on our own knowledge of events, or our sight, for God knows what is best and how to get us where we are to go.

This is restated again in Jeremiah 29:11 (AMP) where it says, "For I know the plans *and* thoughts that I have for you,' says the Lord, 'plans for peace *and* well-being and not for disaster, to give you a future and a hope." This verse verifies that God only wants good things for us, and knowing this can make it easier to have open trust.

Yet, again this is reiterated in Romans 8:28 (AMP) where it says, "And we know [with great confidence] that God [who is deeply concerned about us] causes all things to work together [as a plan] for good for those who love God, to those who are called according to His plan and purpose." This shows we are not only important to God but that he cares deeply for us. How can you not trust someone who loves and cares so deeply for you?

> WHEN SOMEONE WANTS NOTHING BUT GOOD THINGS FOR YOUR LIFE, THEY ARE WORTHY OF TRUST.

* * *

Scripture reminds us, God lives in our hearts and makes his presence known when we most need him. In Ephesians 3:17 (AMP) it says, "So that Christ may dwell in your hearts through your faith. And may you, having been [deeply] rooted and [securely] grounded in love."

When we trust in God our roots grow in Him and we see and feel Him more in our life. His love starts to become more evident and more visible to us. We are able to see Him moving more in our daily lives instead of only when we look back over our lives. We are able to feel the love within us as we become closer with God. We will start to exude this love as we feel this love. It will even take over banishing the loneliness we feel at times.

* * *

BATTLING FEAR WITH FAITH

In Matthew 9:20-22 of the Message Paraphrase, (a paraphrased version of the bible) it reads as follows: Just then a woman who had hemorrhaged for twelve years slipped in from behind and lightly touched his robe. She was thinking to herself "*if I can just put a finger on his robe. I'll get well.*" Jesus turned-caught her at it. Then He reassured her "Courage, daughter. You took a risk of faith and now you're well." The woman was well from then on.

I love The Message's (a paraphrase of the bible, it shortens and even updates the language of the bible) take on these verses because it shows what she was thinking. All I need is to touch the tip of my finger. *Pure faith*. Faith is the action of being willing to do the unthinkable at the time. The certainty within her faith, which allowed her to act, and she was rewarded. Her reward was complete healing. Trusting not only her instinct but also in Jesus, believing he would see her faith, and with her one simple act reward her for it.

At this time and place, with her Illness, she was shunned. She was not to show her face and was to announce when she was coming through the crowd. Jesus had even told her it was due to her courage she was well. She took a risk putting it all on the line because she knew deep in her heart, her gut, with merely a touch she could be healed. She did not ask for it, she simply put her faith into action and went out and did it. Taking the first step was putting faith into action. I find it so interesting this story is only two verses long, yet it has had such a big impact. Who she was is a mystery because if you look into these stories, in each of the multiple gospels, this woman's name is never mentioned. Who she was we will never know, but she was worth mentioning. So much so she is mentioned in three of the Gospels. It is such a small story with such a big message, a message which needs to be heard by everyone.

Taking the first step may be scary but it is so rewarding. Due to courage and taking the first step she was rewarded.

TRUST VS. FAITH

What is it you are looking to God for? What do you need to give you the courage to step out? Is it faith, trust, or certainty?

Even though it can seem scary and difficult, we need to step out in faith and trust because even though we do not see the next step God does. God can see where to direct you and will point you or even push you in that direction. Though this may be after He sees us take the first step, showing we trust him to show us the next ones.

This is discussed in Proverbs 3:5 (AMP): where it says, "Trust in *and* rely confidently on the Lord with all your heart. And do not rely on your own insight *or* understanding."

This is just as the unnamed woman did. She trusted with her full heart, and all she was, trusting Jesus would heal her. With one touch of his clothing, nothing more, nothing less. A simple touch. She did her part leaving her house unannounced, wading through a tight crowd, not saying a word, reaching out she trusted. Jesus did the rest, he rewarded her for her trust.

* * *

Another story which shows the reward of great trust can be seen in the calling of the disciples.

In Matthew 4:18-20 (AMP):

> *As Jesus was walking by the Sea of Galilee, He noticed two brothers, Simon who was called Peter, and Andrew his brother casting a net into the sea; for they were fisherman. And He said to them "Follow me [as My disciples, accepting Me as your master and teacher and walking the same path of life that I walk], and I will make you fishers of men." Immediately they left their nets and followed him [becoming His disciples, believing and trusting in Him following His example.]*

In this story the disciples left everything, their career, their families, all without a second thought. They fully trusted, and with this they got a first row seat to all of the teachings. They were right there and received everything. They were the first to fully trust Jesus. With the trust and willingness to leave everything, their trust granted them a once in a lifetime opportunity.

* * *

This is what trusting God can do for you. It can completely change your life. It can bring a new meaning to life you did not see coming. Trusting God with your life can bring a new light and purpose to your life. As with myself, I always saw myself as a nurse. I enjoyed writing as a hobby, something fun to do or to release my emotions. I never imagined I would come close to writing a book. Yet here I am doing just that. Like I said, God will change your life in ways you could never imagine. Trusting in God is an immense challenge, but it can bring such rewards. The examples above show the type of reward God gives to those who trust and have faith in him. The woman healed, though she was shunned by her community. The disciples lived and learned first-hand from Jesus and were His most trusted companions.

God is asking us for a relationship, and He wants our trust and faith to be in Him. As with any friendship or other type of connection, this goes both ways. We have to be willing to trust if we want God to trust us in carrying out the plans He has for us. To show God we trust and have faith in His plan, though it may be difficult, we must move out of our comfort zone and take the steps we feel compelled to do. These can be things we feel drawn to and cannot shake. Taking these steps are difficult and scary, but the reward can be beyond your imagination. I encourage you to take these steps.

Chapter 7
Faith vs Fear

Fear is the opposite of Faith. To have faith is to be ready to challenge fear each day. To have faith is to believe in things which are not seen or felt with our five senses. According to Hebrew 11:1 (NKJV) that is exactly what faith is as it states, *"Now faith is the substance of things hoped for, the evidence of things not seen."*

The Message Bible (paraphrase) puts it as, "The fundamental fact of existence is that this trust in God, this faith, is the firm foundation under everything that makes life worth living. It's our handle on what we can't see." Having faith is simply believing and trusting in things we are not able to see or even fully understand. With faith it can help us conquer the fears which may hold us back. This verse shows a belief and trust in God alone which is an act of faith; as we are believing in things our senses are not able to make sense of. With God being unseen, though we can experience Him in many other ways, remains unavailable to our natural senses. Therefore, as we believe and trust in Him we exercise faith, and as we see God work in our life faith grows.

Since we are unable to experience God with our natural five senses, it may challenge us in how we experience God. I know personally how my own fear has stopped me from being able to move where God has wanted me to go. Fear puts blinders or a form of glasses on us which causes us only to see the fear or what could happen. They are an impediment preventing us from seeing the possibilities of what God may have for us, or the way in which He may be directing us. For example, when we are being the most challenged this could be Satan trying to hinder us from the abundance which is waiting for us. He is able to do this all through our fear.

A quote by Pastor Donna Pisani puts this all in such a great light, "Behind your greatest fear is a calling that the enemy does not want to come about." Think about that, what is your greatest fear and what can God do when you take one step past the fear? The courage and faith to take one step is all you need. The faith to say ok God I know this is what you want, and I am willing to do this whatever it may be. Take the steps in faith and courage saying, yes Lord I am going to do this and prove I have faith and trust in you. Take the step, it is only one. Dwell on what it is you need to do to show God, *yes* I know what you want from me. I am going to move out of my fear and into something with you, something so much better.

* * *

As our faith grows there are many parables which come to mind, such as the mustard seed in Matthew 13:33-35. We are asked to have such a small amount of faith. While looking into this parable I was curious what is the actual size of a mustard seed, and why is it considered to be so small. They are less than 0.5 centimeters. Now that is small. Each time I see it I think how it is so hard to have pure faith, faith with no doubt, no questioning, no fear, nothing. A true faith knowing, even understanding, this can happen. To have faith the size of a mustard seed and to know without a doubt God will do it. This is hard because in our society we are taught to question everything and to live in doubt. To live in doubt breeds fear and questioning of the things around us. God asks us to listen and obey, sometimes without question to what He wants.

Though we all question, it is a part of our nature to want to know the answers to everything. One thing which may help hinder these questionings is the truth; God only wants good things and abundance for us.

God wants us to live in pure faith, to know Him and to believe in what He says He will do. Pure faith does not mean we will not have things to hinder us, which may tempt us, or get in the way. To live for God does not stop these things from happening, but it can mean as we talked earlier in Jeremiah He has wondrous plans for you. To know this without a doubt is the first step to living with mustard seed faith. The faith which knows God will pull through for you. As you continue to persist within this framework, and consistently see God working in your life, your faith will grow. The ball is in your court so to speak. Yes, He may help you to increase your faith as he reveals himself to you, but your faith is essentially up to you.

In Luke 17:5 the disciples asked Jesus to increase their faith. We may do this daily wanting to have more faith and trust in God. Though this is not something God does, we must do this.

To do this we have to nurture and feed ourselves with His word. Without the proper sustenance we would be much like the Parable of the growing seeds in Mark 4. For as the seeds which were not sown on healthy soil did not produce much fruit (faith) those which are not sown on the healthy and sturdy ground of conviction will not grow well or produce more faith either. We have to nurture and help our faith to grow before we can expect to have a fruitful and continually increasing harvest of faith.

When it comes to faith another story which comes to mind is one we looked at in chapter six, but which is well worth looking at in another light, is the woman who bled for 12 years. This woman does not have her name mentioned, but the faith and trust which she had to be healed was enough to remark on multiple times. She took steps, *literally*. She walked out of her home into the world to find her miracle. At this time due to her illness she was most likely confined to her home. Whenever she went out she had to announce anywhere she went she was unclean, so people would know to stay clear of her. Yet this time she pushed the fear, most likely embarrassment, or even shame (having to announce herself) aside. She pushed her way through the crowd and did not follow the protocols. She made sure she was going to get to Jesus and nothing was stopping her.

Just as fear can block us from Jesus or even from accomplishing what we feel pulled to by God, shame or embarrassment can do the same. The fear, shame, or embarrassment of what family, friends, or even society thinks can hinder or stop the progress we need to be making. It can prevent the good planned for you, getting in the way of what God wants for us. It can be hard to step out and announce our plans to the world, as any of the above can stop us and paralyze us from finding the happiness and joy which we deserve, but the world and the way they see things are not the way God views them. When we share what we want to do, or how we feel, having been directed by God, society may be like *no* that is not what you need to be doing. But just as the woman did not let "what others thought she should be doing" stop her from getting to Jesus, we should not let this stop us from getting to our God given goal either. Fear may wear many different faces, but regardless of how they appear they will all blind us from what or where we are going. As smoke or fog can get in the way, and disorient us from our path, the world may lead us off onto the wrong path without our even knowing it. We may even be following our own path, a path of our own choosing, but this may not be the path which will be the best for us.

* * *

In Luke 17:5&6 (AMP) where it talks about a mustard seed of faith it specifically says, "The apostles said to the Lord,

FAITH VS FEAR

"Increase our faith [our ability to confidently trust in God and in His power]. And the Lord said "If you have [confident, abiding] faith in God [even as small] as a mustard seed, you could say to this mulberry tree [which has very strong roots], Be pulled up by the roots and be planted in the sea'; and [if the request was in agreement with the will of God] it would have obeyed you." This says right here God cannot increase our faith, we have to. We have to have faith in God. To grow our faith we need to trust God. We need to spend time with our Father and get to know Him. How can you have faith in someone you barely know? But to grow our faith we have to also stay focused on God. If we lose that focus then we begin to sink.

In the story of Peter walking on water in Matthew 14:30, as Peter started to look at the world around him, and he saw the storm around him, Peter was seeing through the blinders of fear, he lost his focus on Jesus and he began to sink. We need to spend time with Jesus daily. Staying focused on His words and His promises to us so we too do not begin to sink. If we lose our conviction however, and cry out to Jesus, He will be immediately there to reach out and help. He doesn't dawdle. The longer we keep our focus however, the more we grow in our faith, and the less the world scares us. The less fear creeps in, and the more faith we have in God, then the

> HE IS ALWAYS THERE WHEN WE CRY OUT, THE MOMENT WE LOSE OUR WAY.

more you can stay centered and do what God has planned for your life. What are you seeing in your world through fear? What smoke is clouding your judgement? Do you feel as though you may have taken a wrong path? God will direct you in the right way, for we are attracted to the good which is God. The good is the direction God has for us, but fear will prevent us and have us not see it as good. It will blind us to the reality which is before us, and prevent us from seeing it as God does. What do you believe God's path for you may be?

* * *

In Matthew 14:25-26 (AMP) the disciples were filled with fear, And in the fourth watch of the night (3:00-6:00a.m.) Jesus came to them walking on the sea. When the disciples saw Him walking on the sea, there were terrified and said, "It is a ghost!" and they cried out in fear.

This is a great example of how even those closest to Jesus can be manipulated by fear, seeing things differently because of it. This shows how fear can distort our sight, but in Matthew 14:27 (AMP) He reminds them it is Him when he says, "... take courage it is I!, Do not be afraid." Not only did he then immediately put their fear to rest, He reminded them where to have their sight and courage. To know it was Him and in Him. They needed to be confident, and to feel secure. He told them to take courage and not be afraid. As we have discussed many times in this book taking a step forward in faith can and usually does come with many fears. But we are learning to battle fear with faith. So, this is why I love these words when Jesus tells us to take courage. *To take our fear, to cast it aside and replace it with courage from him.* So, He knows that there is fear involved with getting out of the boat. He knows there is fear in stepping out of what we know and stepping into Him. With this stepping out of the boat and coming to Him comes much fear, but much faith will follow if we can do this. While doing so we have to forget to look at the world around us. Take that step out of what we are familiar and comfortable with. We have to know God will be there for us at all times. As soon as we ask, with faith and trust, we can be more relaxed in stepping out of what is comfortable.

We have to take our courage from God knowing He has the best plan for us. When we do this, and take that step, we are seeking God's plan for us. To have courage in these things

FAITH VS FEAR

is in many ways showing God we trust and have faith in His plan. In doing anything out of our normal, or the little box we have made our comfort zone, we show courage. When we show up for what is in store, we display faith in God to direct us and to be there for us. As we work on our faith and trust in God we show courage. We are continuing our growth with God and our faith. The longer we stay in the boat, the more we stagnate in our faith and the less we will grow. We will become more complacent with where we are and will be more willing to sit there looking at the world around us saying ok, this is my life. But it is not your planned life, God has bigger and better things for you. Step out in faith. Use those spiritual muscles and continue to grow to be more and more like God having faith in the plan He has set forth for you.

Chapter 8
Stepping Out in Faith

Stepping out in Faith can be scary and it can fill your life with fear, real fear. This is holding you back because in a sense it is a new fear, fear of the unknown, asking, "Is God really going to come through for me, or does He have a real plan for me?" It can overwhelm us, and when this happens it is time to look at where we are versus where we were. It is time to look back at what God has done. Looking back into your life you can see the times He has pulled you through.

In Deuteronomy 32:4 (AMP) it says, "The Rock! His work is perfect, For all His ways are just; A God of faithfulness without iniquity (injustice), Just and upright is He."

This scripture shows us when we stand with God we are standing on a solid surface. His ways are solid and moral, and when we follow His ways they become our ways. We start to uphold His values and exhibit his conduct. We start to emulate our Father's behavior or values. What we are taught is what we learn and show the world.

In Jeremiah 29:11, this verse shows God has a plan for you. Not a bad plan for you, but of good, and a future of hope. The (NIV) says it like this Jeremiah 29:11: "For I know the plans for you," declares the Lord, "plans to prosper you and not to harm you, but to give you hope and a future."

STEPPING OUT IN FAITH

To achieve these plans which the Lord has for us, we have to trust and have faith He will follow through believing He loves us and truly wants what's best. If we take a step in faith He will show us the way to go. He truly wants this for you. God does not like to see his children suffering, but we will continue to suffer in fear the longer we hold our full self from our Father. For our father (God) wants all of us and when we surrender all of us to Him, and begin a relationship with Him, His abundance is revealed to us. Surrendering ourselves is stepping out in faith to him saying, take my life and make it yours, for we know He knows best and will give us the best.

* * *

My story is also about stepping out in faith. I had no idea how to write this book, but I knew I needed to write it and simply started. Once I took the first steps, and once I truly committed to writing the book, things started falling into place. The right publisher came along shortly after I committed to writing the book, and I was given the time to put it all into practice with confidence. God really showed me what to do and gave me peace as I stepped out in each way. He gave me the peace and supplied the time and information I needed to bring things together. Once you step up and out, God will provide the way for everything else. He knows the plans he has and the best way to have them come to fruition.

* * *

We see in the story of Peter and the boat a huge example of faith. This story is in Matthew 14:25, (Mark and John). In this story Jesus is walking on water to his disciples on a boat. The first thing Jesus says to his disciples is to take courage and to not be afraid. God knows stepping out in faith can be full of fear. Stepping out of our fear takes determination. Notice how Jesus says *take* courage, not *have* courage. This implies we should take what we lack from Him. We may not have the courage to do things yet, but He has all we need. What Peter says next is fascinating. Peter says to Jesus "If it is you Lord tell me to come to you on the water." And Jesus tells him to come. So, Peter being the obedient disciple he is, gets out of the boat. Now pause for a moment and just think of the fear which has to be running through Peter. He has to be thinking to himself, *don't tell me to come, what was I thinking*. The scene around him is waves crashing and wind howling, and what does Jesus do? He simply tells Peter to come. With pure faith Peter steps out of the boat and starts to walk on water to his master. He does what everyone believes to be impossible. Peter walks on water toward Jesus, eyes fully on Jesus, demonstrating his full faith in his master. He catches a glimpse of what pure faith can do. We do not know how far he got, but he had enough faith to get out and get started. Notice what happens however when he looks around at the world. He gets distracted and he starts to sink. Because of his distraction he loses faith and becomes afraid. Fear and losing faith in Jesus made him begin to sink. As soon as he began to sink, Peter cried out to Jesus to save him and Jesus immediately reached out his hand to him. He did not wait to see if Peter would regain faith, but rather He immediately reached out to him. Jesus is there for us whenever we cry out to him. Though He did ask why Peter doubted, and called him of little faith, Jesus was still there for him. He picked Peter up and they both got back in the boat. Jesus did not scold or yell at him, He simply asked a reflective question. A question we should all ask ourselves from time to time. Why do we doubt? Why do we look at the world and forget our faith because of our fears? Why do we have so little faith in a God of miracles, of love and of faith? We often appear to have so much faith in ourselves or others, but little in God. When God is the one who has provided us with these things we have.

* * *

He is a faithful and strong Father. He is our Rock in the hard times, but it should not be only in the hard times.

In Deuteronomy 32:4 (NIV) it says, "He is the Rock, His works are perfect, and all His ways are just. A faithful God who does no wrong, upright and just is he." This verse shows us so many things. It shows us how strong God is by comparing him to a rock. Think about a foundation, who can break a strong foundation? How much pressure does it take to break that foundation? This shows God is able to handle many things from us, just as a house's foundation can handle much, God is able to as well. Then it tells us all His works are perfect, which means us, among other things. We are His work, us as His children, as humans. It also means our lives. Your life may not seem perfect to you; as I see it my life is far from perfect too. I am not doing what I always pictured myself doing, but God has a plan for me as He does for you. Your potential life is perfect from His perspective, and will go according to His plan if you give it to Him.

This verse also shows God is faithful. We have a faithful loving Father. A Father who thinks you are perfect and a faithful father who has wondrous plans for you. You simply have to see it and step out of fear and give your Father a chance. A chance to guide you through the life He has waiting for you. So, what is tugging at you? What do you feel God pulling you to do? Have you made a commitment to do this thing? What is holding you back? What fear do you have to confront?

When we take these steps there is such a great reward for us. We ensure we are going to make strides in the way God wants us to go and work on the things He has put in our hearts. God has such an abundant life planned for us.

In John 10:10 (AMP), it says "The thief comes only in order to steal and kill and destroy. I came that they may have and enjoy life, and have it in abundance, to the full till it overflows." This shows God has always wanted us to not simply live life but to enjoy it and live it abundantly.

Abundantly, I love this word because it shows not only are we to enjoy the life which is set out for us, but we are to have more than plenty of everything. We are to exude everything we enjoy as it pours out of us. Knowing God wants this for me brings a smile to my face. It warms me knowing He loves me so very much.

* * *

Remember, to have this we must have that all crucial relationship with Him. If we neglect to have a connection with Him, then we miss this step. Taking the initiative to have a relationship with God is the First step to accomplishing any of this. God created us for this purpose, but to have a successful relationship, we need to be willing to hear some things we don't want to such as a redirection in our life. It could simply be God has better things planned for us which will take us in a different direction than the way in which we are currently going.

The willingness to listen and follow will help, but this can be difficult as there may be many unknowns in this new direction. The trust we have in God and His plan for us will help us through, and is what can bring about the abundance.

In Luke 9:23 (AMP) Jesus talks about what it takes to follow Him when He said,

> *"If anyone wishes to follow Me as My disciple, he must deny himself, set aside selfish interests, and take up his cross daily [expressing as willingness to endure whatever may come] and follow me, believing in Me, conforming to My example in living and if need be, suffering or perhaps dying because of faith in me."*

STEPPING OUT IN FAITH

This verse is describing how we have to be prepared to not only be flexible and willing to change course in life; we also have to be willingly selfless and take up our troubles daily. We have to be inclined to make the choice each day to follow God and put our life in God's hands. I am not saying things will always be easy; we will make sacrifices, as this verse says. We will have to sacrifice things, ourselves, our desires. The life God has planned is so much better than what we think we want, which may feel good for a little while but, the plan God has for us is good for us always. We may not always see the good, and may only see the struggles at times, but when we lean on God's word and learn from God we can start to take the next steps. The more we take these steps, the more we learn and start to grow our trust in our relationship with God.

As we step into this relationship we will long for him, and want to know the next thing He has planned for us.

In Jeremiah 29:13 (AMP) it explains, "Then with a deep longing you will seek Me and require Me as a vital necessity and you will find me when you search for Me with all of your heart." This scripture declares when we are with God, as with any other connection, we have a deep longing to be with Him. To desire Him and His presence is totally normal. To want to learn more and draw closer each day is what He wants us to strive for. So, each day as we choose to learn more, and to take steps in harmony with Him, we show our commitment to Him. As we continue to step out each day it becomes more necessary for us to talk to God regularly. When we do this, with pure intent, God will open up the ways for us and show us His path. He won't leave us to find the answer on our own. It may not be on our time-line but He will give us an answer.

> WHEN WE SEARCH WITH ALL OF OUR HEART, HE IS THERE TO ANSWER US.

This can be seen in Psalms 27:14 (AMP) where it says, "Wait for and confidently expect the Lord; Be strong and let your heart take courage; Yes, wait for *and* confidently expect the Lord." So, not only are we to wait and know God has a time for everything. We are to be confident in knowing He will come through for us. So, yes, this relationship requires a lot of patience and trust. It is not easy, but it becomes easier if we take these steps each day. Waiting on Him, knowing, and expecting Him to come through for you, is what builds the relationship. When we choose this daily, it becomes easier. Granted the beginning is not easy, but it is something which will allow the life which God has planned for us to begin to unfold.

Chapter 9
Faith in the Daily

We have talked about what it means to step out in our faith. It can be difficult to take the first steps. Once we take that step however, it not only becomes easier, but as we see the results of our choice we have the desire to do more. To take more steps and to continue to pursue the good which is in God. In Matthew 5:6 (AMP) it says, "Blessed [joyful, nourished by God's goodness] are those who hunger and thirst for righteousness [those who actively seek right standing with God], for they will be [completely] satisfied." This verse declares, the more we lean on God the more we will become satisfied in our lives. The more we lean onto God's goodness; the more we will hunger for more goodness. As we search and work for this goodness, working within this framework, we will become more satisfied.

We can do this by reading His word, learning who God is, and what makes up God. Learning to live in God's love and acceptance, and leaning on the understanding of God. Leaning on the belief in what He knows are his great plans for you. When you truly believe in what God has planned it releases a lot of pressure off of you. You are able to worry less with more trusting in the process of life.

* * *

In Proverbs 3:5-6 (AMP) it says, "Trust in and rely confidently on the Lord with all your heart And do not rely on your own insight or understanding. In all your ways know and acknowledge and recognize him, And He will make your paths straight and smooth [removing obstacles that block your way.]" These verses show God has a path for your life. When we rely on God, we will be directed in the way in which we should go. Verse 6 mentions how God will make our path straight and smooth when we recognize Him. He will remove the big obstacles but not because it will make life easy. It only means He will direct us, still giving us the chance to make our own decisions, still allowing us to make mistakes. Getting through those mistakes and finding our way is easier however when we lean on God; relying on Him to show us the way we are to go.

What does it mean to rely on God? How do you do this daily and trust Him completely? First is to know the character of God and who He is. We have talked about how God is love. 1 John 4:8 (AMP), states, "The one who does not love has not become acquainted with God [does not and never did know Him], for God is love. [He is the originator of love, and it is an enduring attribute of His nature]." As this verse shows, God is love. We learn to love from Him, it is a part of us, and we were given this attribute from God when He created us. We love and desire love as it is all from Him.

He also has many other positive qualities which we should strive to have, to be like our Father. Such as in Psalms 108:4 (AMP), "For your loving kindness is great *and* higher than the heavens; your truth *reaches* the skies." So not only is He love, but He is kind and truthful. Though at times the truth may not be what we want to hear, it is what corrects us and helps us to stay on the appropriate path. He will give us the truth and direct our path with his kindness and love. He will always guide us in the truth and what we need to know.

Many people see God as an angry father, but many times this is not true. I can think of three different times where it mentioned when God was slow to anger, Psalms 103:8, Psalms 145:8, and Proverbs 15:18. Each of these verses talk about how God is slow to anger but full of compassion, love, and kindness. God is merciful, forgiving, and gracious. Knowing these qualities to be of God, how could we not want Him in our lives. With all of these great qualities how can we not see the positive things in our lives from God. The more we search for goodness, the more we see God.

To continue to have faith in our daily life we need to be able to see the blessings which happen to us regularly. The more we keep account of these blessings, or things to be grateful for, the more it can raise our faith. It can encourage us to seek God more and to find more goodness. The more we see His plan the more we desire to live out His plan. To live in His plan we need to live in a relationship with Him. We need to discover His goodness and His love.

* * *

Another thing which can help us see God and have faith in Him throughout our life is to recognize how omnipotent, God is. When we realize how big God is, how all-knowing God is, it becomes easier to recognize His plans, and to have faith in our daily life. It becomes easier to trust in God's plan for our life. Then we can see God in everything. God not only sees all but He created all. He knows the path He has for us is the best, but He chooses to give us free will. Between His goodness and omnipotence there is so much working for us if we are accepting of His plan. How can we not trust and have faith in what God has for us when He is all of these things. These are things we want and strive for in our lives, and God is the example which we follow.

When we see all of these things so frequently in our lives, seeing the positives continually happening for us, we should take account of these things. This way we are able to continue to remember His blessings and how many times in our lives

He has helped us. How many times has he prevented us from taking wrong turns. All those times when nothing else could explain the way in which things worked out. Remembering, and taking all of these blessings into account, brings about the desire to have more; bringing more goodness into our lives. Write them in a journal, list them some place where you can see them. Make this a regular practice so you can often be reminded when, at times, He feels far away. It reminds us of how much God is really there for us.

The more we dive into the word of God, and His teachings, the more we learn of His goodness, and the more we will want to take time to learn of God. This becomes a cycle; a cycle of love. A cycle of love brought on by a God of love.

* * *

We learn to love because God loves us, no matter what we have done or what we will do. God loves us as we are and for who we are. This is what love is, and this is where faith starts by, accepting and loving ourselves, God and God's people. For our faith and trust to grow, we must learn the teachings of God. His teachings show this love and show the ways in which we should conduct ourselves.

> WE LEARN TO LIVE IN FAITH DAILY WHEN WE LEARN TO LIVE IN LOVE DAILY.

As we learn these things, we obey them. As we obey these teachings, we are showing God how much we have faith in what He has taught us. The more we take these steps in faith and step out each day, we show obedience. In Psalms 119:66-68 (AMP), it says, "Teach me good judgment (discernment) and knowledge, For I believed and trusted and relied on Your commandments. Before I was afflicted, I went astray, But now I keep and honor Your word [with loving obedience]. You are good and do good; Teach me Your statutes." There is so much packed into these few verses.

The first thing to look at is how it mentions God is good and does good, which is why we desire to learn from Him and to be like Him. When we learn His ways and are taught through His word, we not only see His good nature, but we learn to do His good as well. Having been taught His good, and by obeying His good ways, we are showing obedience. We are showing how we take steps each day to be more and more like Him. When we continue in this, trusting Him and relying on Him, we see how we have gone astray and have more desire to leave that behind and move forward.

Secondly, when we learn and show obedience, we can do so out of our love for God. When it is done out of love we are showing our faith in His ways. When we do so with all of our heart and our lives, we are showing the love and devotion we have is pure. That this is our choice is what God has always wanted. He gave us free will to make a choice. To choose to have a relationship with Him because we want it. When we use our freedom and choose to follow Him it makes Him abundantly happy. As we follow in this decision we are choosing His goodness and to be within His goodness. As we step out in faith this shows our obedience and our love for God's ways.

Also, being obedient is a way of showing our faith in our daily lives. As we continue to follow God's example of goodness and unconditional love we are learning more about Him. As we learn more about Him we become more like Him. The more we are like Him, and we uphold and obey what He has shown us, the more we are showing our love for Him. We show Him our love by being faithful and obedient in loving Him and His people. Remember God is love and His example is of goodness.

With the obedience comes Trust, and as we obey and continue to see His goodness, it becomes easier to Trust. Trusting God and believing in His word can be easier when we see what He has done for us. But also trust in God's word and He will be there in any way we need Him to be. As it says in

His word, Psalms 112:7-8 (AMP) "He will not fear bad news; His heart is steadfast, and trusting [confidently relying on and believing] in the Lord. His heart is upheld, he will not fear while he looks [with satisfaction] on his adversaries." So as we look at these verses we are shown how, yes, bad news may come, or should I say will come, but when we rely on God we can remain positive only good is meant for us. For one because we have seen it many times in our own past, and also because God's word has told us this many times. An example which comes to mind is Jeremiah 29:11. We have looked at this verse many times, with both Jeremiah and Psalms 112 verse 8 telling us we need not fear and our heart will remain upheld.

Fear is meant to stop us, to make us want other things, to put us on hold. But when we rely on God we will be upheld, and we will be satisfied no matter where our adversaries may be. It does not matter where others think we should be, for we will be satisfied when we rely on God. When we take that step each morning and decide to obey God and depend on God, we'll be satisfied in where we are going.

Philippians 4:6 -7 (AMP) states, "Do not be anxious or worried about anything, but in everything [every circumstance and situation] by prayer and petition with thanksgiving, continue to make your [specific] requests known to God. And the peace of God, [that peace which reassures the heart, that peace] which transcends all understanding, [that peace which] stands guard over your hearts and your minds in Christ Jesus [is yours]."

This shows just how God can communicate with you and let you know you are on the right path. That peace which you cannot explain is God residing in you and directing you. You communicate when you obey and listen. If we do not open the connection on our end by talking through prayer, and by obedience, stepping out each day in faith, then we shut down this communication. When we shut it down, we can become lost. To stay on the path where we want to have these lines of communication open, we must obey, talk, listen, and keep our relationship with Him alive. We take a step-in faith each time we do these things out of our love and commitment to God.

So, let's do this, let us live a life on our own path, through faith with God, listening to His loving guidance and obediently and lovingly following His ways. His ways which are good and loving.

ACKNOWLEDGMENTS

To my wonderful husband who has believed in me from the start. Who pushed me to continue to write and stay on track, encouraging me to chase my dreams and follow my heart. And to the family who has supported me and encouraged me through each obstacle along the way.

ABOUT THE AUTHOR

Amber is a mother of two with a Bachelor's in psychology after 11 years as a nurse, she has become a life coach, helping many through the ups and downs of everyday life. She is now fulfilling her life passion of writing and helping others.

LOOK For the Devotional to Follow.
A GUIDE to Help you Step By Step to go alongside this book

For a more intense work through, work with Me to get past your fear. You can find this information at www.adviseversa.com, to come soon.

www.ingramcontent.com/pod-product-compliance
Lightning Source LLC
LaVergne TN
LVHW011739060526
838200LV00051B/3252